What Your History Books Failed To Tell You

by

Azeem Hopkins-Bey

authorHOUSE™

1663 LIBERTY DRIVE, SUITE 200
BLOOMINGTON, INDIANA 47403
(800) 839-8640
WWW.AUTHORHOUSE.COM

First published by AuthorHouse 12/20/04

ISBN: 1-4208-1043-X (sc)

Library of Congress Control Number: 2004098581

Printed in the United States of America
Bloomington, Indiana

This book is printed on acid-free paper.

Acknowledgements

I GIVE PRAISES TO ALLAH AND HONOR TO PROPHET NOBLE DREW ALI, AND ALSO TO THE FORERUNNER MARCUS GARVEY. I GIVE HONOR TO ALL THE TRUE AND DIVINE PROPHETS JESUS, MUHAMMED, BUDDHA, CONFUSCIOUS, etc. (PEACE AND BLESSING BE UPON ALL THE PROPHETS OF ALLAH). I EXTEND HONOR TO ALL WHOM HONOR IS DUE. I EXTEND HONOR TO ALL THINGS PERTAINING TO ISLAM.

Dedication

This book is a dedication to you the reader. If you are reading this book you are trying to gain understanding of who you are. Knowledge is power, and if you don't have true knowledge of yourself you don't have any power at all. This book is used to aid and assist in the study of Prophet Noble Drew Ali's teachings, and not to come in conflict with Prophet Noble Drew Ali's teachings. Nor is this a substitution for Prophet Noble Drew Ali's teachings.

IN LOVING MEMORY OF MY BELOVED BROTHER

HAKEEM RAHMAN HOPKINS-BEY

Table of Contents

I extend high honor to my mother and father (Sis. Sueann Hopkins-Bey & Bro. Ronald Hopkins-Bey). They truly demonstrated p.3 of The Holy Koran of the Moorish Science Temple of America. They prepared me early with instruction, and seasoned my mind with the maxims of truth. They watched the bent of my inclination, and set me right in my youth, nor did they let an evil habit gain strength with my years. My parents are both Sheiks/ess, and Divine Ministers. They have been members of the M.S.T.of A. since the early seventies. My parents are true scholars of Moorish Science. In fact chapter 1 of this book comes from my father's October 14th trek back in history pamphlet. They have instructed all 8 of their children (myself being the 7th) with the lessons of Prophet Noble Drew Ali. The Holy Koran of the Moorish Science Temple of America teaches that "He who hath as many children hath as many blessings," and "it is upon thee also that dependeth whether the child of thy bosom be a blessing or a curse to thyself." My mother and father are the proud parents of 8 children, 23 grandchildren, and 1 great grandchild. My father always taught me that the smallest nation is a family. I extend high honor to my father (Master Accountant/ Historian) for he has the wisdom and knowledge of the ancients. I studied in his library at home since the age of 12; books such as, Stolen Legacy, Babylon to Timbuktu, Sex and Race, Ohaspe, Osirus, Isis Unveiled, The Moors of Spain, Golden Trade of the Moors, Golden Age of the Moors, Othello's Children in the New World, etc. I am blessed to be under his tutelage. I extend high honor to my mother (Master Herbologist/ Children Sunday School Instructor) for she has the love of angels. She has taught me the Holy Koran of the Moorish Science Temple of America while in the womb. Anytime I have been sick; I never had to go to the hospital for she could find the herbal tea that healeth me. I hear their praise with a secret delight. Happy is the children that call them parents.

I extend honor to my brothers and sisters; for each one of them individually have helped to inspire me to write this book. Adriene, Twanna (Qiyamah), Ronnie, Terrance, Hakeem, Tahira, and Shambram (Sheikess) who has truly been of tremendous assistance to me in completing this work.

I extend honors to my nieces and nephews; Bahiya, Nashid, (lil) Terrance, Hakeem, Rashaun, Haneefa, Latif, Rafi, Ali, Mecca, Fatima, Rahman, Hanee, Idrees, (lil) Ken, Ronald III, Quoyasia, Ismal, Khalif, Khalil, Khary, (lil) Shambram, Faheem, and my great niece Aniya.

I extend honors to the whole Hopkins/ Caldwell family. I extend honors to Sis. Elisa Herder-Bey (my best friend) who has been a tremendous help to me in completing this work. I extend honors to my Grand Sheik of Temple #11 Bro. Khatib Marifa-El and to the entire Sheik board. I extend honors to the Grand Governor of the state of Pennsylvania Bro. J. Brown-Bey. I extend honor to the national Grand sheik of the M.S.T. of A. Inc. Bro. R. Jones-Bey, and to his official staff. I extend honor to all whom honor is due.

Chapter I
"Trek back in history", History of the slave marks Negro, Black, Colored, etc. by Ronald Hopkins-Bey Sheik/ Divine Minister of the M.S.T. of A. Inc.

Often times we pick up history books looking for the truth of the so-called black man of America. We have come to the conclusion that he stems from a nation of kings and queens, but what happened to this nation of kings and queens. Why are the progeny of this nation of kings and queens in the state that they are in? The Holy Koran of the M.S.T. of A. teaches that, *"Through sin and disobedience every nation has suffered slavery, due to the fact that they honored not the creed and principles of their forefathers. That is why the nationality of the Moors was taken away from them in 1774 and the word Negro, black, and colored was given to the Asiatics of America who were of Moorish descent, because they honored not the principles of their mother and father, and strayed after the gods of Europe of whom they knew nothing."* The type of slavery we are suffering from today is mental slavery, due to the fact of our nationality, and birthrights being taken away in 1774. We often read about the literal shackles that were put on the so-called black man and women of America, but very rarely do we read about the mental

1

shackles that were put on, and still exist in the minds of the so called black people in America. The key to this conspiracy begins with question #85 of our Koran Questions for Moorish-Americans; each question in the Koran Questionnaire has a story or a history attached. Question #85 states; "*Name some of the marks that were put upon the Moors of the Northwest by the European nations in 1774? The answer states, Negro, Black, Colored and Ethiopia.*" Through identifying with these slave marks of Negro, Black, Colored, and Ethiopia, the Moors after many generations forgot the true national name of their forefathers, therefore cutting themselves off from being a nation of people, and the illustrious history of their forefathers. The beginning of this historical event occurred September 5th 1774 in the state of Pennsylvania in the city of Philadelphia (the first capital of the United States of America).

Moorish American History

COMMANDER OF THE AMERICAN ARMY, 1775 PRESIDENT OF THE UNITED STATES, 1779

GEORGE WASHINGTON SAID, "I TELL NO LIE, THAT I CHOPPED DOWN MY FATHER'S CHERRY TREE"

On September 5th 1774 the Moors were a divided, and defeated nation here in North America. On that date, the 13 European colonies or nations met in Philadelphia in a building known as Carpenter's Hall. It was a Masonic convention. Masonic is defined as pertaining to or characteristic of freemasons or freemasonry (secret society with secret passwords, hand shakes, and secret ceremonies with meanings only known to their members, and secret signals). The meeting or convention was originally called the Odd Fellows Convention. The popular name of this convention according to the European history books became known as the First Continental Congress, and George Washington was elected chairman of the convention. In Masonic terms he was elected Grand Master.

Two of the main issues, which were discussed, and debated were: (1) how were the 13 colonies going to form a united front against King George III of England. (2) How were the 13 colonies going to justify the institution of perpetual slavery of the Moorish in habits, and population, (whom were renamed by the European nations with names such as Indians, Negroes, Blacks, Colored's etc). Now issue #1 was to form a united front against King George III of England; the 13 colonies voted to draw up a treaty between themselves, because the 13 colonies were actually 13 separate nations or countries at that point in time. This treaty or document became known as the Articles of Confederation in your history books, and this had solved issue # 1. Issue # 2 which the delegates debated at the convention was to justify perpetual enslavement of the Moorish population. The 13 colonies agreed to strip the Moors of their nationality, and birthrights; which was an act of European psychology. The European colonist gave the Moorish population the slave marks of Negro, Black, Colored, Ethiopian, etc., and the European colonist defined these slave marks as something inferior to the name white. The European colonies defined white as a color of purity, and defined black as representing everything of evil. White and Black was also used as a legal status;

white meant that you were a citizen, and Black meant you were not a citizen. When the Moorish population accepted the inferior slave marks of Negro, Black, Colored, etc. the Moorish inhabitants cut themselves off from the illustrious history of their forefathers whom were the founders of the first civilization of the old world.

The Moors' forefathers did not form the slave marks of Negro, Black, and Colored etc. These inferior names or identities marked the Moors as inferior class of beings whom had been subjected to slavery. The marks or slave names would forever disqualify and rob Moors from being a free person (citizen) in the true sense or meaning in which the term free person (citizen) is used in the Articles of Association, Articles of Confederation, The Declaration of Independence, The Northwest Ordinance of 1787, and the present day Constitution of the U.S.A.

The strategy of the plan or conspiracy of the Europeans which they used is as follows: If the Moors were ever emancipated or set free in the future; the Moors would remain subjective or dominated by the European race whom had the sole authority in the

CARPENTERS' HALL:

The meeting place of the First Continental Congress: The slave names(marks)of Negroes, Black, Colored and Ethiopia are given to the Asiatics of America, Whom were of Moorish descent. This was the consensus(agreement)of the 13 Colonies in 1774 A.D.

classifying system via race, and race was incorrectly being distinguished as colors such as Black- race, and White- race. The Moors would unknowingly forfeit their rights to true citizenship. The slave classifying system was designed just for that purpose. Through this method the Moors would not have any rights under the laws governing free national citizens. The Moors known illegally as Black people would rob themselves of the precious rights of citizenship by excepting, and identifying with the slave marks of Negro, Black, Colored people; none of those names pertained to a true nation of people.

The chairman of the convention George Washington summarized the raging debate on how to perpetuate slavery of the Moors with this statement: "If we would agree to take the Fezzes, and Turbans off the Moors' heads and remove the sandals from their feet and enforce it with severe punishments, and to also swear a death oath between ourselves to religiously, and faithfully not to allow anyone to teach the Moorish children whom they really were or who there forefathers were. And only allow the Moorish children to be taught that they were truly Negroes, Black people, and Colored folks; (George Washington) stated that 200 years from today the Moorish people would not know their nationality nor the national name of their forefathers also they would not know from which land or ancestors that they are descended from." The meeting adjourned with a consensus that they would secretly meet again October 14th 1774 at the Pennsylvania State House, which later became known as Independence Hall.

INDEPENDENCES' HALL:

The Moorish Flag; The Proverbial Cherry Tree. History records this as the "Chopping Down Of A Cherry Tree" by George Washington; The First President of the U.S.A..The Moorish National Flag was first hidden in a secret vault at Independence Hall in 1774 A.D.

The 13 colonies or European nations convened at the Pennsylvania State House, which is now known as Independence Hall, on October 14th 1774 and adopted the document known as the Articles of Confederation (published in 1778), and the marks agreed upon on September 5th 1774. The Bible was used as a source of reference to justify the European nations color classification system, which was used to enslave the Moors. They used the Old Testament of the Bible chapter Genesis. Genesis chapter 9 verse 25 dealing with the curse of Canaan states, ***"And he said (Noah) Cursed be Canaan; a servant*** *of servants shall he be to his brethren.* " The European nations also declared they were fulfilling a prophecy found in Psalms chapter 83 verses 4 & 5 where it states, *"come, and let us cut them off from being a nation","they are confederate against thee,"* which is the document known as the Articles of Confederation.

Philadelphia was the first capital of the U.S.A., and was also an ancient strong hold of the Moors of the Northwest before 1774. The Moorish Flag flew here before the year of 1774; the Moorish flag is over 10,000 years old, the mother of flags. The Moorish flag is a red flag with a five-pointed green star in the center. The proverbial "cherry tree" which history records George Washington saying, "I tell no lie that I chopped down my fathers cherry tree" which symbolized our Moorish national flag and nation. The Moorish flag, after being forbidden to fly here in America, was first kept in a secret vault hidden in Independence Hall, then it was moved to New York the 2nd capital of the U.S.A. and finally moved to Washington D.C. the present capital of the U.S.A. Our Moorish National Flag remained in a secret vault for over 100 years until the coming of Prophet Noble Drew Ali to whom all honor is due. He retrieved our Moorish Flag, and forced the president of the U.S.A. at that time to return the Moorish national flag with its five-pointed green star in the center, which was missing for centuries. This event occurred between the years of 1913 and 1925.

Our brother, the Moroccans' five-pointed green star was not displayed in their flag until the year of 1956; after winning their independence from France.

There is another landmark in Philadelphia near Independence Hall where the Liberty Bell resides. There is a Biblical inscription on the Liberty Bell dealing with the Hebrew law on slavery (Leviticus 25:10). This law was given to Prophet Moses on Mount Sinai to proclaim liberty throughout the land unto all inhabitants. Abraham Lincoln used this particular chapter of Leviticus to oppose Christian slaveholders. Lincoln was also trying to appeal to the slave master's religious consciousness. The slaveholders (whom the majority of them were Christians) were using Genesis chapter 9 verse 25 to justify the enslavement of the Moors where it states, *"a servant of servants shall he be to his brethren."* The word servant was interpretive by the European nation as meaning slave. The European slave masters knew our Moorish history, and also that our ancestors were Canaanite-Moabite; which was to be kept a secret. Only until the coming of Prophet Nobel Drew Ali (to whom all honor is due) were these secrets finally brought to light.

The Holy Koran of the M.S.T. of A. states, *"The inhabitants of Africa are the descendants of the ancient Canaanite from the land of Canaan."*

LIBERTY BELL:

President Abraham Lincoln used Leviticus 25:10, to oppose Christian slave-holders, from perpetuating the enslavement of the Moors. The Leviticus 25th Chapter served as the basis for the 13th amendment to the United States Constitution 1865 A.D..The inscripted statement on the Liberty Bell "PROCLAIM LIBERTY THROUGHOUT THE LAND UNTO ALL INHABITIANS"

11

Chapter II
European Psychology and the use of the slave marks.

We have just trekked back in history, and received a lesson on how, and why the slave marks were put on the so-called black people of America. Now we have to come up to modern times to see how these slave marks are still affecting the so-called black race psychologically. We know through the passing of the 13th amendments that neither slavery nor involuntary servitude shall exist within the United States except as a punishment for crime whereof the party has been duly convicted. Even though slavery was abolished in 1865, we still see the effects of the slave marks in the year 2004. In this chapter, we will thoroughly define the slave marks that we are still clinging to since 1774; in this we will see clearly the European psychology that was formed to keep "the sleeping giant" from arising. The sleeping giant is symbolic for the great nation of Moors who civilized mankind.

All throughout the years since the United States government came into existence, identity has been misplaced by race. Race is a classification of modern humans formerly based on an arbitrary selection of physical characteristics. A German anthropologist by the name of Johann F. Blumenback (1752-1840) started these early classifications of race. He classified race in three categories

Caucasoid, Negroid, and Mongoloid. These were the predecessors to the now black, white, red, yellow, and brown races, which are incorrectly being used to identify human beings.

Prophet Jesus said, ***"My words and deeds in all the walks of life shall be the proof of my Messiahship."*** Each word that we speak carries a particular vibration into the ethers. It can carry either a positive or a negative energy. If we use negative words to identify ourselves, often times we will manifest it's meaning in our actions. The very words we use to identify others and ourselves could be the one thing keeping us from developing the greatness that is in each and every one of us. For instance, if your child is identified as an idiot from birth, to puberty, to adulthood; your child will grow to be the best idiot he or she can be. Even if the child tried they would not be able to develop the highest in them, because an idiot is defined as someone who is mentally deficient; therefore he would not be challenged with the same lessons of the average child. Thus, the child would be praised for succeeding on a scale that is below average, because of his or her status. The same refers to the person identifying himself or herself as a black man or a black woman. Dr. Pimienta-Bey said ***"a person calling themselves black trying to make it positive is like pushing a elephant uphill on roller-skates."*** If you do not know yourself then you leave the authority to someone else to identify you, and through time you will be accustomed to that label.

Black is an adjective; which is a descriptive word, and not a noun. A noun is a person, place, or thing; therefore a person cannot be black. Black is defined as gloomy; pessimistic; dismal (a black future); sullen or hostile (black words); harmful; evil; wicked (a black heart); indicating censure or disgrace (a black mark on a persons record); marked by disaster or misfortune (black areas of drought); AFRICAN-AMERICAN; to lose consciousness or memory temporarily. Black according to science means death. Black is also a color, and colored means anything that has been painted, stained, varnished, or dyed; therefore a person cannot be black. Black and colored have all been used to name the olive hued person or their descendant. Colored, now somewhat old fashioned, is often offensive, it is still used, however in the title of the National Association for the Advancement of Colored People. In the late 1950's black began to replace Negro and is still widely used and accepted. Negro is a name given to a river in West Africa by Moors because it contains black water (the Negro river is located in what is called today South America "Brazil").

When one tries to find the origin of the term Jim Crow, it was thought that he was a slave from Cincinnati Ohio; others say he was from Charleston, South Carolina. Another faction holds that Jim Crow derived from old man Crow, the slaveholder. A final group says that the Crow came from the simile, black as crow. Whatever the case, by 1838 the term was wedged into the language as a synonym for Negro. Thus, "Jim Crow Laws" meant Negro laws. Black Codes were laws passed by certain southern states after the Civil War with the intention of limiting the freedoms of so-called black people. The South developed new laws to recreate the old "slave codes" laws that pretended to protect so-called blacks, but in fact restricted their activities. These new "black codes" were almost identical to the slave codes; in most cases the word "slave" was replaced with the word "black" or "Negro". That is the reason why the Sundry free Moors of South Carolina had to clarify their legal status in the years of 1789-1790. They new being identified as Negroes, blacks and colored folks they would be subject to the black codes which were slave laws; therefore they had to proclaim their nationality, identifying themselves as Moors subject to a prince in alliance with this government (see, Journals of the House of Representatives, South Carolina 1789-1790). By clarifying their legal status as Moors they were automatically placed under the jurisdiction of the longest unbroken treaty between the United States of America and a foreign government, The Peace and Friendship Treaty of 1787 between Morocco and the U.S.A. Under this treaty it is illegal for Moors to be placed as chattel property. Treaty's along with the Constitution of the U.S.A. are the supreme law of the land.

People identify themselves as black due to ignorance. Ignorance is lack of knowledge. People don't take the time to look up definitions of words; every word has a meaning, if it doesn't have a meaning its not a word. People call themselves black due to acceptance also, accepting any name given to them such as Negro, black, colored, and African-American, instead of doing the research to see who they truly are. Acceptance is also a sign of passive-ism. There are three states a person could be in at any time, and they are passive, assertive, or aggressive. When it comes to your identity you should never take a passive approach.

White is also an adjective, which is a descriptive word; therefore a person cannot be white. White is defined as pure; morally pure; lacking malice; harmless (white magic); a person whose racial heritage is CAUCASIAN; top grade. During the first census taken in 1790, if you were a citizen you were classified under white person, because white and black are also political statuses. White means you are a citizen; black means you are not. When you look at the definitions you will see the psychology. When you see the term black you see things pertaining to negativity, and then you see African-American. When you see the term white you see thing pertaining to positivism, then you see a person whose racial heritage is Caucasian.

People call themselves white, because it is convenient. It is easy to be identified with something that pertains to positivism. Some people are ignorant of the fact that a person cannot be white. I have never seen a white person in my life! We have to realize this racial classification system is an instrument to create an inferior and a superior race. Several people try to use the term Caucasian to designate persons instead of the term white, but many people don't know that Caucasian is just as bad as using the term white to designate persons. Caucasian is defined as: of designating or characteristic of one of the traditional racial divisions of humankind; of the Caucasus region, its people or their culture; a person having Caucasian physical characteristics. Caucasian comes from the word Caucasoid. Caucasoid is one of the three categories created to separate mankind on the basis of physical characteristics. The other two categories are Negroid and mongoloid. The so-called black races are Negroid, the so-called white race is Caucasoid, and the so-called yellow, red, and brown races are mongoloid. The word Negro and "nigger" are derivatives of the word Negroid; therefore if you call a person a Caucasian he or she has the right to call you a Negro or "nigger".

In ancient times people did not classify races according to skin complexion, like modern nations of Europe and America. The ancients including the Greeks and Romans identified people according to their national or tribal names. They used such names as: Visigoths, Vandals, Saxons, Carthaginians, Arabs, Persians, Babylonians, Egyptians, and Moors. They did not use terms such as: Negro, black, colored etc. (which are modern terms) to refer to the olive hued races; or the term white and Caucasian to refer to the European nations. We have to realize that race really deals with physical characteristics, and that is not correct when identifying human beings.

Chapter III
Nationality and its Function

When it comes to identifying humans we have to look to nationality. Nationality is defined as national quality or character; the fact of belonging to a particular nation; separate existence as a nation; national independence or consolidation. In the definition where it speaks of national quality or character it shows relevancy to the suffix –ish. The suffix –ish forms adjectives that pertain to a nation. It is defined as the sense of belonging to a person or a thing; of the nature or character of; having the qualities of. For instance, Scottish-American or Turkish-American. The nationality Turkish-American denotes that the persons nature, quality, or character is that of Turkish origin or decent, and he or she is born or naturalized in America.

Everybody in the United States of America has a nationality, but everyone is not conscious of his or her nationality. The way to identify a person's nationality is by looking at their last name. We are incorrect by identifying persons by skin complexion and physical features, which are race. It is only through nationality that we may be correct in identifying human beings. These are some examples of how last names denote national origin; Ibn Saud-Arabian; Pavlov-Czechoslovakian; Robertson-English; Aristides-Greek; O'Brian-Irish; Fitzgerald-Norman; McDonald-Scotch; Petterson-Swedish; Petrowski-Polish; Romanovitch-Russian; Bey-Moorish. A persons name is the most prominent feature to others than their most intimate friends. It is also a person's most vulnerable point. An old Latin maxim runs *"sine nomine homo non est"* (without a name a man is nothing) especially a national descent name. A persons name is their signboard to the world. It is one of the most permanent possessions; it remains when everything else is lost, and it is owned by those who possess nothing else.

Serial No.118. (Resolution No.75). Printer's No.1034.
By Mr. WITKIN.

MOORISH-AMERICAN SOCIETY OF PHILADELPHIA AND USE OF THEIR NAMES.

In the House of Representatives, April 17, 1933.

Many sons and daughters of that proud and handsome race which
Inspired the architecture of Northern Africa and carried into Spain
The influence of its artistic temperament have become citizens of
This Nation.

In the City of Philadelphia, there exits a Moorish-American
Society made up of Moors who have found here the end of their
Quest for a home, and of the children of those who journeyed here
From the plains of Morocco.

This Society has done much to bring about a thorough absorption
By these people of those principles which are necessary to make
Them good American citizens.

These Moorish-Americans have, since being here, missed the use
Of the titles and name annnexations that were so familiar at home and
Which are used in accordance with the doctrines of the religious
Faith to which they are adherents; therefore be it.

Resolved, That this House commends the Moorish-American
Society of Philadelphia for the efficient service it has rendered
The nation in bringing about a speedy and thorough americanization
Of these former Moors, and that in accordance with the fullest
Right of religious independence guaranteed every citizen, we
Recognize also the right of these people to use the name affixes—
El, or Ali, or Bey, or any other prefix or suffix to which they have
Heretofore been accustomed to use or which they may hereafter
Acquire the right to use.

Laid over for printing, April 17.
Adopted, May 4.

In the Senate
Referred to the Committee on Corporations, May 4.

Honoring the Moorish-American Society of Philadelphia.

WHEREAS, The Moorish-American Society of Philadelphia is a thriving vital community made up of Moors who have sought a better life and brighter future for their children as they journeyed here from the desert plains of Morocco; and

WHEREAS, The Moorish-American community has readily adopted the principles of freedom and democracy so necessary for their assimilation into the larger family of Americans from all manner of ethnic, religious, cultural and racial backgrounds; and

WHEREAS, These Americans, who hail from a proud and ancient culture whose influence in philosophy, architecture and the arts has helped define North African culture for centuries, have become productive, involved and contributing members of the American system, yet loyal to the doctrines of the religious faith to which they are adherents; and;

WHEREAS, The Moorish-American community recognizes assimilation as fundamental to becoming full Americans, yet also seeks to maintain the flavor of their cultural roots by the use of titles, prefixes and suffixes which have been the custom within this dynamic culture for centuries; therefore

RESOLVED, BY THE COUNCIL OF THE CITY OF PHILADELPHIA, That we hereby recognize the rich, artistic and creative aspect of this unique community. We give full allegiance to those constitutional guarantees of religious independence which will enable citizens of Moorish descent to carry on those traditions so vital to the definition of their presence as a people by the use of the name affixes El or Ali or Bey and that this recognition is accompanied by the highest respect for the Moorish people and their culture.

RESOLVED, That an Engrossed copy of this resolution be presented to representatives of the Moorish-American community as evidence of the profound respect and sincere admiration for the contributions made to this city by Moorish-Americans.

CERTIFICATION: This is a true and correct copy of the original Resolution adopted by the Council of the City of Philadelphia on the twelfth day of September, 1991.

Joseph E. Coleman
President of City Council

Introduced by
David Cohen

21

A name is the only efficient means of describing a person to his contemporaries, and to his posterity. When one dies it is the only part that lives on in the world. Ancient philosophers believed that the nature and character of things were condensed and represented in their names hence "nationality".

Nationality is important, because constitutional rights pertain to citizenship, and citizenship pertains to nationality. There is a direct correlation to citizenship, and nationality. A person lacking a nationality does not have the rights of a citizen; they have granted privileges. therefore a person lacking a nationality is not a citizen. For instance in the 1960's so called black people were fighting and marching for the constitutional rights of citizens. The constitution was adopted in the year of 1789. The constitution pertains to the rights of citizen. The black man or women is unconscious of his or her nationality; therefore being unconscious of his or her nationality he or she is not a citizen in the true sense of the word. In the 1960's Civil Rights were enacted due to lack of constitutional rights. We have to realize if you were a citizen in the true sense of the word there would be no need for alternative rights or granted privileges to spring up. Prophet Noble Drew Ali stated, ***"The citizens of all free national governments according to their national constitution are all of one family bearing one free national name. Those who fail to recognize the free national name of their constitutional government are classed as undesirables, and are subject to all inferior names and abuses and mistreatments that the citizens care to bestow***

***upon them. And it is a sin for any group of people to violate the
national constitutional laws of a free national government and
cling to the names and the principles that delude to slavery".*** That
is why in the 1960's (100 years after slavery) so called black people
were treated as if they were below a human is because they failed to
recognize the free national name of their constitutional government;
therefore they were classed as undesirables, and was subject to all
mistreatments, misuses, and abuses that the citizen cared to bestow
upon them.

Now you may ask yourself why were the so-called black
people being treated in such a manner irregardless of the fact that
the constitution guarantees rights to citizens, and the 14th (1865)
amendment makes the so-called black man a citizen, and the 15th
(1865) amendment allow voting rights . The (so-called) black man
didn't receive voting rights until the mid 60's, and that was in fact a
granted privilege which can be revoked at any time. That is because
the 14th and 15th amendments to the constitution have nothing to do
with the so-called black person. Prophet Noble Drew Ali said ***"the
14th and 15th amendments brought the North and South in unit
placing the Southerners who were at that time without power, with
the constitutional body of power, the free national constitutional
law that was enforced since 1774 declared all men equal and free,
and if all men are declared by the free national constitution to be
free and equal since that constitution has never been changed,
there is no need for the application of the 14th and 15th amendments
for the salvation of our people and citizens".*** The Prophets words

23

echo with truth. There was a General by the name of Robert E. Lee. He served as General of an army who fought on the side of the Confederate states during the Civil War. By fighting on the side of the Confederate states he forfeited his rights to U.S. citizenship. When the war was over, and he was released from jail, General Robert E. Lee had to apply for citizenship. In 1865 Lee signed the Amnesty Oath required in order to apply for citizenship. By the passing of the 14th and 15th amendment it made the transition from non-citizen to citizen smooth for the Southerners who were at that time without power. There were over 300 people from Mississippi alone that had to apply for citizenship through the 14th amendment via the Amnesty Oath. The so-called black person has to proclaim a free national name to be recognized by the government in which they live and the nations of the earth. By identifying with the slave marks of Negro, Black, Colored, etc. you rob yourself from the precious rights of citizenship.

Nationality determines the political status of the individual. Political rights derive from political status. Political rights are the rights of citizens established or recognized by constitutions, which give them the power to participate directly, or indirectly in the establishment or administration of government. If you don't have a nationality you have no political rights nor status. Nationality is also used as opposed to territoriality for the purpose of distinguishing the case of a nation having no national territory. For instance there once existed a land called Palestine; you cannot find that land on the map today. Today that land is called Israel. The P.L.O. is the Palestine

Liberation Organization; they are preserving their nationality through a corporation even though Palestine is not on the map. The function of the M.S.T. of A. is similar to the P.L.O.; the M.S.T. of A. preserves the nationality of the Moors. Act 6 of the Divine Constitution and By Laws of the M.S.T. of A. states ***"With us all members must proclaim their nationality and we are teaching our people their nationality and their Divine Creed that they may know that they are a part and a partial of this said government, and know that they are not Negroes, Colored Folks, Black People or Ethiopians...."*** One function of nationality is to transfer a nations history, culture, land, etc. from one generation to another, if one generation becomes unconscious of their nationality they have become unsuccessful in transferring all those great gifts.

We have to truly come to grasp that African-American is not a nationality. African-American is a misnomer for the Moors of America. If you observe the order of the United Nations; you will see no African representative or nationality. You may see Uganda; Morocco; Egypt; Sudan, or Algeria etc. Africa is composed of many nations. If you were to meet a person from the Sudan, he will not accept the misnomer African-American, because he is conscious of the fact that he is Sudanese-American. If you were to meet a person from Egypt he would never accept the misnomer African-American even though Egypt is in Africa. African-American, black, colored, and Negro are all misnomers for a people who were stripped of their nationality in 1774. The true nationality of these people is Moorish-American. The Declaration of Human Rights states that everyone has a right to a nationality; no one shall be arbitrarily deprived of his nationality.

Chapter IV
Moorish- Americans, Who are they?

The true nationality of the so-called black person is Moorish-American. The so-called black person must proclaim the nationality of his ancient forefathers. *"There is no one who is able to change man from the descendant nature of his forefathers...."* The Moorish were the ancient Moabites, and the founders of the Holy City of Mecca. Moabite breaks down to Mo-ab-ite; which translates to "mo" a semetic term meaning from; "ab" a Semitic term which means father similar to "abu" in Arabic which means father (Abraham- father of many nations), and –ite is a suffix which means tribe. The Moabites are the tribe or nation that comes from the father, and Allah is the father of the universe, (The human seed that came forth from the heart of Allah....[Holy Koran of the M.S.T.of A.]). Moor is short for Moorish. The term Moor in medieval times was used to designate individuals who were phenotypic ally Africoid. Some individuals try to categorize Moor, and black as synonyms, but they are hardly synonymous. The only characteristic a Moor has in common with a (so-called) black person is physical features. The (so-called) black person is a slave, and the Moor is not. You'll notice derivatives of the term moor through the different languages of the world. In the romance languages (Spanish, French, and Italian) of medieval Europe, Moor was translated as Moro, Muir, and Mor. Even in the present, the Spanish word for blackberry is mora- a noun that originally meant Moorish women. Also in Spanish, the adjective for dark-complexioned (olive hue) was Moreno, but it currently means brunette. In French moricaud means dark skinned (olive hue) or blackamoor, while morillon means black grape. In Italian mora means Moorish female, while moraiola means black olive.

CITY OF PHILADELPHIA

Proclamation

Morocco was the first nation to recognize the independence of the United States of America, establishing a Peace and Friendship Treaty between the two countries in 1787, which has been the longest unbroken treaty in this country's history.

The Moorish-American Society of Philadelphia has existed in this city for many years, being a thriving, vital community of Moors who have sought a better life and brighter future for their children by journeying to the U.S. from the desert plains of Morocco.

On July 20, 1928, exactly a year before he died, Noble Drew Ali, a Moorish-American, legally established and incorporated the first Islamic religious organization to appoint and consecrate missionaries (Sheiks) to propagate the faith of Mohammed in America, thus establishing the Islamic faith in America.

THEREFORE . . .

I, John F. Street, Mayor of the City of Philadelphia, do hereby proclaim Friday, July 20, 2001 as

MOORISH-AMERICAN
INDEPENDENCE DAY

in Philadelphia, in recognition of the contributions made by Noble Drew Ali, and in respect of the manner in which Moorish-Americans maintain their belief in God (Allah) as their forefathers and express their loyalty to their adopted country of the United States.

JOHN F. STREET
Mayor

Given under my hand and the Seal of the City of Philadelphia, this twentieth day of July, two thousand and one.

Why is the so-called black person a Moorish-American? Because the so-called black people are descendants of Moroccans and born in America. Don't be scared! We are not saying that all so-called black people come from Morocco. The Moabites were driven out of the land of Canaan by Joshua Ben Nun, and received permission from the Pharaohs of Egypt to settle in a portion of Egypt. In later years they formed themselves kingdoms, and one of the kingdoms was Morocco. Therefore the so-called black man was a Moor even before the founding of Morocco, thus saying Moroccan is just a modern term for Moabite. A Moor can trace his line genealogy all the way back to the Garden of Eden, because the Moabites (the ancestors of the so-called black race) were the founders of the Holy City of Mecca, and the modern name for the Garden of Eden is Mecca.

Morocco was a Moorish rock; a foundation for which later became an empire. The dominion and inhabitation of the Moroccan empire extended from North-East and South-West Africa, across the great Atlantis even unto the present North, South and Central America and also Mexico and the Atlantis Islands; before the great earthquake which caused the great Atlantic Ocean. Thus saying the so-called black people of America are the progeny of the Moors who were subjects of the Moroccan empire. The Holy Koran of the M.S.T. of A. teaches that, ***"What your ancient forefathers were, you are today without doubt or contradiction"***. The so-called black people of America are Moors who were stripped of their nationality and birthrights.

Chapter V
The truth about Islam, and sectarianism in Islam.

The so-called black man was stripped of his nationality and birthrights in the year of 1774. The so-called black man has no true birthrights, because your birthrights derive from your creator. The Declaration of Independence states that you are endowed by your creator with certain unalienable rights; that among these are life, liberty, and the pursuit of happiness. The so-called blacks mans religion was taken away from him in 1774; therefore he had no knowledge of his true creator. The so-called black man was forbidden to practice his religion, and forbidden to call on his true creator, which is Allah. The true religion of the so-called black man is Islamism. Islamism is the faith or doctrine of Islam. Islamism was the first religion, or way of life of the world (living the life of peace). The very nature of the creator Allah is peace. The religion of Islamism was instituted by Allah for mankind. The whole point of our existence is to be perfected in the sight of Allah; to make our way back to Him. The shortest distance between two points is a straight line, and that straight line is Islamism; the straight and narrow path. Since Islamism was instituted for mankind from the beginning, and ALLAH DOES NOT CHANGE HIS MIND, HIS MIND IS MADE UP FROM THE BEGINNING, the religion that He instituted then is the same religion we are to follow today.

The religion of Christianity was not brought by Jesus. Christianity did not exist during the time of Jesus, and he did not come to bring a new religion; he brought the religion of his forefathers (Noah, Moses, Abraham, etc.)The followers of Jesus were known as disciples. The term Christian did not come into existence until Paul, and Barnabus entered the city of Antioch (Bible-Acts 11:26), and that was after Jesus was crucified. The word Christian comes from the word Christ which is a Greek word which means anointed. Jesus was raised amongst Jews, but Jesus was not Jewish, Jesus disputed with the doctors (learned men) of Jewish law at the age of 12 (Holy Koran of the M.S.T. of A. Ch.5)(Bible-Luke 2:45-49). He disputed with them, because he was teaching the true and divine creed of Islam, and the Jewish teachings were contradictory to Islam. The foundation of Christianity began in Rome; the term Christian was coined in Antioch. Jew comes from the name Judah; Judah was the son of Jacob; Jacob was the son of Isaac; Isaac was the son of Abraham, and Abraham was neither Jew nor Christian, because those religions did not exist then. Abraham was an upright man, a Moslem (Quran 3:66). Whatever has been made will be unmade; that which begins must end. Islam has no beginning, and it has no end.

Islam is an Arabic word which means submission (submission to Allah). Islam derives from the root word Salaam, which means peace. Islam is preeminently the religion of peace. Islam is a very simple faith. It requires man to recognize his duties toward God Allah, his Creator and his fellow creatures. It teaches the supreme duty of living at peace with ones surroundings. The goal of a man's life according to Islam is peace with everything, peace with Allah, and peace with man. The Quran, the holy book of Islam, tells us that the final abode of man is the "house of peace" (Quran 10:25) where no vain word or sinful discourse will be heard. The holy divine prophet Noble Drew Ali says that a follower of Islam in the true sense of the word is one whose hands, tongue and thoughts do not hurt others. Buddhism is connected to Buddha, Confuciusm is connected to Confucius, Christianity is connected to the "Christ", Zoroastrianism is connected to Zoraster; Islam is different from all other religions, because it connects you directly to the creator of all, Allah. Islam is the first religion. All the true and divine prophets brought Islam to the people; it is only after the prophet passes form, the people go off the path. Jesus, Muhammed, Buddha, Confucius, Noble Drew Ali, Abraham, Moses, Zoraster etc. all brought Islam. The principle of Islam is the oneness of Allah and man, and peace with everything. All the prophets brought the principle, but people will not comprehend that, because the prophets also brought different customs according to the needs of the people of that particular time and space. Men come to Allah through ceremonies and forms, which are customs, but customs do not alter the nature of truth, nor can the opinion of man destroy justice. A follower of Islam is called a Moslem. A Moslem is simply a person who submits to the will of Allah, so essentially all prophets were Moslem. The greeting of a Moslem is either Islam (which means peace) or Salaamualaikum (which means peace be unto you). The greeting of the Prophet Jesus

was Peace be unto you (Holy Bible, John 20:19), and the language
he spoke was Aramaic, which Arabic and Hebrew derives. When a
Moslem serves the creator of all Allah, he serves his kin, those who
are no kin, the stranger at his gates and the foe who seeks to do him
harm. A Moslem believes that when man harms in thought or word
or deed another man, he does a wrong to Allah; when man honors
man he honors Allah, and what man does for man he does for Allah.
Moslems also believe that Allah's meeting place with man is in the
heart, and in a still small voice he speaks, and he who hears is still.

Prophet Muhammed was the founder of the uniting of Islam.
Muhammed received the divine revelations, which brought forth
the Quran. The word Quran is an infinitive noun from the root
"qara'a" which signifies primarily he collected together the things;
the secondary significance of the root word is reading or reciting a
book. The name Quran really refers to both the root-meanings, for
on the one hand it signifies a book in which are gathered together all
the divine books, a distinction to which the Quran itself lays claim
(Quran-98: 3), and elsewhere on the other hand, it means a book
that is or should be read. Prophet Noble Drew Ali says it should be
read whether considered from a literary, religious, or philosophical
point of view. There are thirty-one different names under which
the Quran is spoken of in the revelation itself, the most important
of these being "al-Kitab" - the book, and "al-Dikr" - the reminder.
The Quran was revealed on the lailat al-Qadr or the Grand night or
the night of Majesty (Quran-97: 1), which is a well-known night
during the month of Ramadhan. By the revelation of the Quran in

the month of Ramadhan is therefore meant the commencement of its revelation. The month of Ramadhan is thus a memorial of the revelation of the Quran. Quran in blacks law dictionary is defined as a book containing ecclesiastical and secular law. Prophet Noble Drew Ali said we have it as the revealed word of God Allah. The Quran itself is the basis of knowledge and instruction, for it is Allah's words and guidance (Quran-2, 2). The M.S.T. of A. derives their power and authority from the great Quran of Muhammed. The great Quran of Muhammed is not to be confused with the Holy Koran of the Moorish Science Temple of America. The Holy Koran of the Moorish Science Temple of America was not given to take the place of the great Quran of Muhammed. The Holy Koran of the M.S.T.of A. is the everlasting gospel; it is the saving power that comes from Allah through our ancients fathers by his Prophet. The only savior of the world is love, and Jesus has come to manifest love to men. Within the Holy Koran of the M.S.T.of A. is the missing 18 years of Jesus life which is not present in the Holy Bible. Page 3 of the Holy Koran of the M.S.T. of A. states *"these secret lessons are for all those who love Jesus and desire to know about his life works and teachings"*. The true (Injil) gospel of Jesus is present within the Holy Koran of the M.S.T.of A. In essence the lessons of The Holy Koran of the M.S.T.of A. were in existence prior to the revelation of the great Quran of Muhammed, because the Moslems of India, Egypt, and Palestine had the lesson, and they kept them back from the outside world until the time was appointed by Allah that these secret lesson were freed and delivered into the hands of the Moslem of America by Prophet Noble Drew Ali. The great Quran of Muhammed gives credence to the spiritual lessons revealed before it, (Quran 35:31 ***"An d that which We have revealed to thee of the Book, that is the truth, verifying that which is before it. Surely Allah is Aware, Seer of His servants.)*** (Quran 2:41, 2:89, 2:101, 5:48, 6:93)

Islam is the fastest growing religion in the world. Every since the coming of prophet Muhammed, the religion of Islam has been spreading at an astounding rate. Islam is a natural way of life. There is a well know misconception that Muhammed spread Islam with the sword. There should be a distinction made between the Muhammed of 570-632 A.D., and the Muhammed of 1453 Byzantine. Muhammed of 1453 who was of Turkish descent spread Islam with the sword. Muhammed of 570-632 A.D. who was of Arabian descent recited Quran to the people; upon hearing the Quran the people would weep and also convert due to the beauty, eloquence, and truth of what they heard. Muhammed used his sword to protect himself against unbelievers who wanted to kill him, because he professed what seemed to them as new. The religion Muhammed brought is a tolerant religion.

The religion of Islam is the most misunderstood religion in the world. This misunderstanding most of the time comes through individuals who do not demonstrate the religion of Peace brought by all the divine prophets. This misunderstanding comes from individuals demonstrating ideals of men. These ideals of men come from the different sects that were formed after the passing of prophet Muhammed in 632. These divisions occurred primarily because of lack of obedience to law (Quran), respect, loyalty to government (Moslem community), tolerance (towards your brothers and sisters), and unity (with your brothers and sisters). The first of these divisions occurred between two groups, one calling themselves Sunni another calling themselves Shiite.

The Sunni tradition is know in Arabic as the Ahl-I-Sunnah (the people of Sunnah), a term which according to the earliest classical sources emerged in the ninth century. The word "Sunnah" means custom, method, path, or example, and refers particularly to the example of the prophet Muhammed as found in Hadith (sayings or customs). The Ahl-I-Sunnah are those who follow the customs of the prophet and his companions in trying to understand the Islamic faith. During the early centuries following the passing of prophet Muhammed, Islamic scholars sought to consolidate, and systemize Islamic belief and practice. One of the challenges confronting Moslem scholars was how to determine which of the many thousands of Hadith (sayings or customs) attributed to the prophet, and his companions were authentic. In the ninth century two men named Muhammed Ismail Bukhari (870A.D.), and Muslim al Hajjaj (875A.D.) collected and sifted through many thousands of traditions in order to compile dictionaries containing the traditions of the prophet. They based their decisions on the reliability of particular transmitters (isnad-train of transmitters). Al-Bukhari and Muslim reduced the massive number of Hadiths (sayings or customs) to several thousand. In the tenth century these collection were given canonical status by the Sunni Islamic community. In addition to these two collections, lesser-known scholars compiled four further collections of Hadith. While regarded as authentic and canonical by the Sunni community, these do not have quite the same status as those of al-Bukhari and Muslim. *(Ibn-Abbas said when the ailment of the prophet {Muhammed} became worse, he said bring for me paper and I will write for you a statement after which you will not go astray. But Umar said. The prophet {Muhammed} is seriously ill, and WE HAVE GOT ALLAH'S BOOK {Quran} WITH US, AND THAT IS SUFFICIENT FOR US. But the companions of the prophet differed about this, and there was a hue and a cry. The prophet said to them go away. It is not right that you should quarrel in front of me).* It was Allah who inspired the Quran and man who inspired Hadith, and the Quran is not incomplete. To institute other books other than the Quran is to say that Allah left something out, and Allah left nothing out. The Quran says in (surah) chapter 2 (ayat) verse 2 *"This Book, there is no doubt in it, is a guide to those who keep their duty,"* (surah) chapter 17 (ayat) verse 89 *"And certainly We have made clear for men in this Quran every kind of description, but most men consent to naught except denying"* (surah) chapter 16 (ayat) verse 89 *"...And We have revealed the Book to thee explaining all things, and a guidance and mercy and good news for those who submit."* (surah) chapter 39 (ayat) verse 27 *"And certainly We have set forth for men in this Quran similitude's of every sort that they may mind".* The Sunni follow any one of four major schools on jurisprudence founded by Imams ibn Hanbal, abu Hanifa, Malek, and el-Shafei; Imams of the ninth to the eleventh centuries. These schools referred to respectively as the Hanbali, Hanifi, Maliki, and Shafei, are followed by different Moslem states either entirely or in part. Egypt is traditionally Maliki. Saudi Arabia is traditionally Hanbali, although the country follows more closely the teaching of Imam Muhammed Abdal-Wahab (Wahhabiyyah), a Hanbali reformer of the early 1800's. While following man you are lead astray unknowingly; while following Allah and his messengers you are always on the right path. In these different schools of thought there are different interpretations of the Sharia (Islamic law).

The Shiite movement dates from the period when a group of Muslims wanted Ali ibn abu Talib, the cousin and son-in-law of the prophet to become the Khalifa instead of Abu Bakr, who had been elected the first Kalifa following the passing of prophet Muhammed in 632. They advanced his candidacy on the basis of heredity. However, they were voted out; Ali ultimately became the fourth Khalifa, succeeding Uthman, who succeeded Umar, who succeeded Abu Bakr. Ali was overthrown by the rebellion of Muawia, the governor of Syria, whose seat was in Damascus. Muawia rebelled against Ali, because he attributed the assassination of his kinsman Uthman to Ali's followers. Ali was assassinated after losing the Tahkim (arbitration) to Muawia. In 680 Hussain, one of Ali's sons led a number of Moslems who were then rebelling against the ruling Khalifa to try to establish in the area between Iran and Iraq a khalifa based on heredity from the prophet. However, Hussain was lured into Iraq, and there at a place called Karbala he and his followers were massacred. Hussein's martyrdom spurred the Shiite movement in

Iran and Iraq. The Shiite population commemorates the anniversary of Kabala every year. In Iran it is conducted by means of a large popular demonstration in which people publicly weep and scourge themselves as a sign of their remorse.

The political rift between followers of the principle election and those favoring descent from the prophet generated some other differences between Sunni and Shiite approaches to jurisprudence. For example the Shiite view the sayings of Fatima (the daughter of the prophet), and Ali (fatima's husband), the fourth Khalifa of Islam, as equally as authoritative as the Sunna of the prophet, the Sunni do not. There were other sects that sprung up such as the Wahabiyyah, the Ahmaddiyya movement, and the Sufi.

The Sufi movement is a mystical strain in Islam, which reflects the need of individuals to transcend formal practices in order to attain higher levels of spiritual fulfillment. Because of its mystical spiritual character Sufism appeals more to individuals and small groups. Sufi's believe they follow the prophet's mysticism, particularly during the Meccan period of the revelations. Thus in their practices there is much meditation and solitary, or group recitations of prayers and incantations of different formulas. They seek a life of pietism, shunning worldly pleasures, and seeking the inward purity of a relationship with Allah through love, patience, forgiveness, and other high spiritual qualities.

In the 20th century there was the emergence of the first Islamic organization in the west, known as the Moorish Science Temple of America. It was founded in 1913A.D. in Newark New Jersey by

Prophet Noble Drew Ali (1886-1929). In 1913 the Moorish Science Temple of America was known as the Canaanite Temple. Prophet Noble Drew Ali said we organized as the Moorish Temple of Science in the year of 1925, then November 29th 1926 the Moorish Temple of Science was legally incorporated as a civic organization; the name Moorish Temple of Science was changed to Moorish Science Temple of America in May of 1928, in accordance with the legal requirements of the Secretary of the state of Illinois. July 20th 1928 the organization was changed from a civic to a religious organization making it the first Islamic organization in America. The purpose of the organization is to uplift fallen humanity. The M.S.T. of A.'s mission statement is to propagate the faith and extend the learning and truth of the great prophet of Ali in America; to appoint and consecrate missionaries of the prophet and to establish the faith of Muhammed in America. The Moorish Science Temple of America is neither sect nor a faction. The members of the Moorish Science Temple of America do not label themselves; the members identify themselves as being Moslem by faith, and Moorish by descent. The Moorish Science Temple of America teaches the importance of nationality, and Islam (National and Divine movement). It focuses on bringing the so-called black person out of mental slavery, and bringing him back within the constitutional folds of law by allowing him or her to proclaim a free national name, and religion making him or her a whole person, and not 3/5 human (Constitution of U.S.A. article 1 section 2). The founder of the M.S.T. of A. Noble Drew Ali was truly a modern day prophet. The Holy Koran of the M.S.T. of

A teaches that *"when the world is ready to receive, lo, Allah will send a messenger to open the book and copy from its sacred pages all the messages of purity and love* (John& Jesus). *Then every man of earth will read the words of life in the language of his native land, and men will see the light, and walk in the light and be the light"*. The Holy Quran says, *"We sent no messenger but with the language of his people, so that he might explain to them clearly. Then Allah leaves in error whom He pleases. And He is the Mighty, the Wise"*(14:4), and (35:24) states *"And there is not a people but a warner has gone among them"*. Noble Drew Ali was truly a prophet of Allah; a Moorish prophet born in the native land of the Moors (America); speaking English so we can receive the message clearly. There are some people who do not consider Noble Drew Ali a prophet, because they read in the Holy Quran (33,40) that prophet Muhammed is the *"seal of the prophets"*(Khatimu 'N- Nabiyin). The word Khatim means "seal". Khatim does not mean last. The Arabic word for last "Akhir". The word seal means something that serves to authenticate or confirm; an attest to authenticity, accuracy, quality, etc. Prophet Muhammed is truly the seal of the prophets, because he serves as the perfect example for mankind as of all the prophets. Prophet Muhammed was also the last prophet of those days, just as Prophet Noble Drew Ali is the last prophet in these days. Allah sends prophets according to the needs and conditions of the people. Allah sends prophets as a mercy for mankind. Prophets not only bring principles of Islam, but they also bring customs. The prophets Adam, Noah, Abraham, Moses, Zoaraster, Jesus, Muhammed,

Buddha, Confucius, and Noble Drew Ali all brought the principles of Islam, but their customs, or ways of worshipping were different. The Holy Quran says *"For every one of you We appointed a law and a way"* (Quran 5:48); the appointment of a law and a way for everyone refers to the giving of different laws or customs to different nations in accordance with their requirements, thus the Quran here recognizes the principle to which it refers to frequently that prophets were raised among every people (Quran 10:47, 13:7, 35:24, 14:4). Prophet Noble Drew Ali did not come to cause confusion, but he has come to clear up the misconception of Allah and man. He put the so-called black person back on the straight and narrow path, not with customs, but with principles. Prophet Noble Drew Ali brought the world Moorish Science. Science is a system of knowledge gained through observation, study, and experimentation carried on to determine the nature or principle of that which is being studied. One function of science is to create order in apparent chaos. We unite science with our religion, and religion with science in order that we may not become superstitious, nor exceed the limits of Allah.

Quran (3,102)- *HOLD FAST BY THE COVENANT OF ALLAH ALL TOGETHER AND BE NOT DISUNITED*.........Quran (6,160)- *AS FOR THOSE WHO SPLIT UP THEIR RELIGION AND BECOME SECTS, THOU HAST NO CONCERN WITH THEM. THEIR AFFAIR IS ONLY WITH ALLAH, THEN HE WILL INFORM THEM OF WHAT THEY DID.*

Chapter VI
Prophet Noble Drew Ali, The great man and his accomplishments.

PROPHET NOBLE DREW ALI (JANUARY 8TH, 1886 -JULY 20TH
1929)

Many people do not realize the major impact this Noble Prophet had on the present civilized world. It is the present history books that are silent to the great deeds of Prophet Noble Drew Ali, who was the predecessor to many of the great accomplishments our race has brought forth. I deem it necessary to submit a brief synopsis of some of the great works of this modern day Prophet. It is the work of this master mind that inspired me to produce this book. Prophet Noble Drew Ali was born January 8th 1886, in Samsonville North Carolina. At the age of 27 he founded the Moorish Science Temple of America in 1913, in Newark New Jersey (the first Islamic organization in America). The purpose of the organization is to uplift fallen humanity. Prophet Noble Drew Ali returned the nationality and divine creed back to the so-called black people of America. Prophet Noble Drew later moved the headquarters of the organization to Chicago. While in Chicago Prophet Noble Drew Ali turned out the first Moorish national newspaper in America; one of America's first Asiatic (so-called black) national newspapers. This newspaper was distributed in 15 different states throughout the United States. Prophet Noble Drew Ali taught that Asiatics (so-called black people) should gain economic security. He said *"no other one thing is more needed among us at this time than greater economic power"*. Prophet Noble Drew Ali established one of the first Asiatic (so-called black) Manufacturing Corporations (which provided jobs for so-called black people), The Moorish Manufacturing Corporation; which continues to produce remedies such as Moorish Mineral and Healing Oil, Moorish Antiseptic Bath Compound, and Moorish Tea. Prophet Noble Drew Ali held a National Conclave October 14th 1928; among those who were in attendance were Alderman Louis B. Anderson, Jesse Binga of Binga state Bank, Oscar DePreist candidate for Congress, Alderman Robert R. Jackson, Daniel Jackson committeeman of the second ward, and representative George W. Blackwell (Richard Ross Bey was the master of ceremonies). Prophet Noble Drew Ali not only gained the respect of the citizens of this country, but also prominent political figures. Prophet Noble Drew Ali endorsed the fist Asiatic (so-called black person) elected into congress in the 20th century Oscar DePriest. All Asiatics were driven out of Congress during the reconstruction period; the last Asiatic to remain was George White, and he was removed in 1901. The were no Asiatic representatives in Congress until the coming of Prophet Noble Drew Ali. Long before the Civil Rights era members of the Moorish Science Temple of America were casting a free national ballot at the polls for Oscar DePreist, under the leadership of Noble Drew Ali. Prophet Noble Drew Ali retrieved the national flag of the Moors; the Moorish flag which is a red flag with a five pointed green star in the center. What makes this deed so significant is that Prophet Noble Drew Ali displayed the five- pointed green star in the center of the flag at a time when the five- pointed green star was not displayed in the Moroccan flag. The five- pointed green star was not displayed in the Moroccan flag until 1956, after winning their independence from France. Prophet Noble Drew Ali was flying the red flag with the five- pointed green star in the early 20's. Prophet Noble Drew Ali was truly a man ahead of his time, but yet he was in time and on time. Prophet Noble Drew Ali came to resurrect the minds of the so-called black person of America. He came to teach him that he is not a Negro, colored person, or black person. He came to teach the so-called black person that he has a nationality (Moorish-American), and divine creed (Islam). He came to put the so-called black person on an equivalent echelon with all of humanity. He came to bring the one true and divine way peace may be obtained in these days, and that is through Love, Truth, Peace, Freedom, and Justice being taught universally to all nations in all lands. Prophet Noble Drew Ali's work is internationally known. In 1986 the ambassador of Morocco Maati Jorio paid tribute to Prophet Noble Drew Ali by attending the Moorish Centennial Celebration honoring Noble Drew Ali. Prophet Noble drew Ali was truly a pioneer. These are just some of the great works he has accomplished. His mighty work should be studied by all, in order to bring humanity to a solid rock of salvation.

SO AFTER READING THIS BOOK,

NOW WHAT DO I DO?

GO OUT AND SEEK THE MOORISH SCIENCE

TEMPLE OF AMERICA INC. FOR A

MOORISH SCIENCE TEMPLE OF AMERICA DIRECTORY

SEE : *www.moorishsciencetempleofamericainc.com*

FOR MORE INFORMATION CONTACT: ***MOORISH SCIENCE TEMPLE OF AMERICA INC. MOORISH SCIENCE TEMPLE #11,***

2259 N. 5TH ST.

PHILADELPHIA PA. 19133

PHONE NUMBER IS (215) 203- 8008 OR (215) 771- 0967

Bibliography-

1) The Holy Koran of the M.S.T. of A., Prophet Noble Drew Ali, 1927

2) Koran Questions For Moorish Americans, Prophet Noble Drew Ali

3) Moorish Literature

4) Holy Quran, Prophet Muhammed, Mulana Muhammed translation

5) Holy Bible, King James Version

6) Oral traditions of the M.S.T. of A.

7) Random House Webster's College Dictionary, Random House New York 1997-second edition

8) Black's Law Dictionary revised fourth edition

9) The Oxford Universal Dictionary, 1902

10) The Story of our names, Smith, 1950

11) The Story of Islam, S.F. Mahmud, 1959

12) Islam. Encyclopedia/html

14) From Babylon to Timbuktu, Rudolph R. Windsor

15) Chicago Defender, newspaper article, Saturday October 13, 1928

16) Prophet Noble Drew Ali Centennial Celebration booklet.

17) Moorish-American Guide To The Historical Area, Philadelphia Pa.

18) United States of America Constitution.

19) Journals of The House of Representatives, 1789-1790, South Carolina.

20) Peace and Friendship Treaty 1787, Morocco and U.S.A.

About the Author

Azeem Hopkins-Bey was born on January 13, 1980 in Philadelphia Pennsylvania. Azeem was 7th of 8 children, raised in a loving Moorish American household. Azeem attended Samuel S. Fels high school and later went on to study at Community College of Philadelphia. He majored in business and political science. He then entered the Adept Chamber of The Moorish Science Temple of America, at the age of 17; where he was granted the title Sheik. He received his Divine Minister papers at the age of 19 and is currently 24 years of age, and the Chairman of Moorish Science Temple #11. He is also a board of director of The Moorish-American Society of Philadelphia Inc.& a member of the Moorish-American unification Council. He also is a member of Men United For A Better Philadelphia. While being a faithful member to his Temple, he also delivered multiple speeches in various locations. He gave one speech at the Community College of Philadelphia and another speech at the Sedgwick Theater, Masjid Muhammed, etc. All speeches pertaining to the teachings of Prophet Noble Drew Ali. Azeem has received many awards from Temple #11 for his outstanding services and industrial acts in the area of uplifting of fallen humanity. In addition, Richard Allen Committee Inc. has also presented Azeem with a plaque as an appreciation for his assistance in feeding the community each year.

CPSIA information can be obtained at www.ICGtesting.com
Printed in the USA
LVOW08s1238030416

481977LV00004B/294/P